No matter your location, your style, or your budget, beautiful design should be available to all. As a pioneer in the digital magazine industry, *Rue* has inspired thousands since establishing their business in 2010. Now *Rue*'s editorial director Kelli Lamb has created this incredible collection to carry their style and advice into book form. *Home with Rue* is a compendium of inspirational and accessible ideas to help anyone imagine, plan, and create their ultimate living space. Visit Rue at www.ruemag.com and @ruemagazine.

HOME WITH RUE

STYLE FOR EVERYONE

HOME WITH RUE

KELLI LAMB

FOREWORD BY NATE BERKUS

TEN SPEED PRESS
California | New York

For my grandma Edith, whose living room was impeccably designed and where I always felt at ease.

And for Danny, a brilliant business partner and an even better friend.

Contents

1 Make an Entrance   5

ENTRYWAYS | It's the neglected space where you kick off your shoes and toss your keys into a bowl. But it can be a whole lot more. They say first impressions matter, and this is the place to show off your personality and set the tone for the entire home.

2 Easy Living   23

LIVING ROOMS | Acting as both a spot to entertain guests and the cozy place where you watch your latest Netflix obsession, living rooms should be elegant and comforting all at once. We explore different living room layouts for different lifestyles.

3 Pull up a Chair   57

DINING ROOMS | Life happens around the dinner table. It's where we connect with our family and friends, play riveting games of *Catan*, and review tomorrow's homework assignment. In this room, form should meet function.

Foreword

I'VE ALWAYS BELIEVED YOUR HOME SHOULD TELL YOUR STORY, and the way you do that is through your things. What we choose to display in our homes is perhaps one of the truest reflections of who we are . . . where we've come from, and where we hope to go. Nothing should cross the threshold of your home that you don't absolutely love. Period.

I've been a reader of *Rue* mag since its first days as a groundbreaking online home publication. The magazine has always showcased people and interiors that are cool, unpretentious, and transformative. I've spent my career giving people permission to live how they want in their homes, and Rue, now helmed by the very talented and visionary Kelli Lamb, has always implicitly understood that, and they have empowered their readers to do the same.

The best homes, just like the best stories, are ones that are deeply personal–and not afraid to break the rules. Brava, Rue–here's to continuing to tell the best, most interesting stories and empowering us to live authentically.

Nate Berkus

Introduction

WHAT DOES HOME MEAN TO YOU? It's a question I've asked hundreds of people in my ten years as an interiors editor. Though I'm usually the one inquiring, I've got an answer myself: *home is a feeling.* To me, home is a sleeping cat in the living room's one sunny patch. It's the clinking of champagne flutes to celebrate a big accomplishment. It's your favorite knit blanket and a new season of *Succession* (or *Real Housewives*) queued up. Home is where life happens, and as we all have learned in the last couple of years, life certainly happens.

Our homes need to be more functional than ever before. With the big shift toward working from home in early 2020, what once was as simple as a "living room" quickly evolved to become a mobile workspace, classroom, and gym. Kitchens reclaimed their role as heart of the home, as we all sharpened our knives and our culinary skills. Our outdoor spaces began to feel like vacation spots, and our entryways were like an old friend, welcoming us back to our own personal safe havens.

If you've picked up this book, I'm guessing you're like me and crave beauty in your everyday routines. Yes, I want my home to be functional, but I also want it to cultivate that feeling. I want my space to energize me, to comfort me, and to bring me joy. The thing is, with each home tour I've shared over the years, I've discovered hundreds (and hundreds and hundreds) of ways to make that happen. Is a functional, joyful home a minimalist space composed of shades of gray or is it an explosion of pattern, color, and texture? I believe it can, and should, be both.

I have done my best to always infuse the pages of *Rue* with that same ethos. Founded in 2010 as one of the first digital shelter magazines, the founding team (which included interior designer Crystal Palecek and designer + content creator Anne Sage) paved the way, sharing beautiful homes and meaningful stories about the people who lived there. With a goal to provide a pathway to stylish living, we created Rue Daily in 2013, sharing fresh content to inspire our readers every day of the week and keeping up with the pace (and attention span) of social media. In 2021, we had our biggest launch yet, debuting our first-ever print issue on newsstands everywhere. Yes, moving from digital to print might have seemed a bit backward, given the state of media today, but we saw a trend among our audience members that we couldn't ignore. There was a craving for something a little slower, a little more meaningful. There's nothing better than putting the screen down and diving into a print magazine or a beautiful book. It's escapism at its finest . . . no notifications popping up in the center of a photo to lure you to another app or article.

If you're new to *Rue* or you've followed it every step of the way, you might notice that we're not defined by a singular look. We feature sprawling coastal estates alongside petite studio apartments. In one issue, you may see a rustic cabin in the woods of Vermont, followed by a colorful French Colonial in New Orleans, and then an urban loft in Paris after that. I believe that you can discover beauty in all of these spaces, even if you wouldn't necessarily copy the *decor*. This "room for everyone" idea is best seen in our popular #HomeWithRue hashtag. In the early days of managing our social media, I noticed more and more folks starting to share photos of their own homes, replicating the style of their favorite designers or experimenting with #shelfies (cute photos of bookshelves) and living room layouts. We encouraged our fans to tag their images #HomeWithRue and have really enjoyed watching the gallery grow. Across the world, people are offering an intimate look into their space, getting feedback from friends, and further identifying what home means to them.

I have always had an interest in interior design but admit my passion is deeply rooted in interviewing designers and homeowners alike. It brings me great joy to understand why certain decisions were made and how the home functions and then translating how our readers might get the same effect in their space. Over the years, I've taken a few design guidelines to heart: there is a specific reason for that exact shade of white paint, scale is important in everything from tile to chandeliers, and, my favorite, most of the "design rules" are meant to be broken.

Consider this book a compendium of inspirational and accessible ideas to help you imagine, plan, and create your ultimate living space. While you won't necessarily find handy DIYs in the pages that follow, you will be given plenty of insight on how to recreate the looks you love from some of the top designers in the industry. *Home with Rue* is basically one big home tour–but it's also filled with images from dozens of my favorite homes we've shared over the years alongside new spaces you'll love. In chapter 1, I'll take you through the entry, sharing savvy tips to make a good first impression or avoid major shoe pileups. We'll continue through every room of the house, from grand dining rooms to functional laundry rooms, ending with a great selection of outdoor spaces. We'll explore different aesthetics: California Casual, Modern Farmhouse, Mountain Chic, Industrial Minimalism, to name a few. My hope is that you'll identify the look you connect with most, discover something new, and snag some tips on how to bring it home.

Mostly, I hope you'll have a clearer understanding: *What does home mean to you?*

Make an Entrance

First impressions matter. A stylish entryway is the quickest way to show your guests (or the UPS person) that you've got great taste, convincing them that just beyond the threshold is your magazine-ready, perfectly styled pad—where there's minimal clutter, carefully fluffed pillows, and great art. A well-organized entry might say "There is definitely not a load of laundry that's been sitting in the dryer for three days." Or another one, outfitted in a bold, tropical wallpaper, could say "Look at what a fun, adventurous person I am!"

Can we rethink that approach, though? When I say "first impressions," the only person your entryway should impress is you. This is the portal from the outside world to your personal sanctuary. An entry welcomes you back after a joyful dinner with friends, a painful trip to the dentist, or spring break at the beach with the entire family. It's the spot your kids come tumbling into after school, and the place where you kick off your heels at the end of a big presentation. It needs to be functional and suit all the needs of your lifestyle, but more importantly, it needs to welcome you home.

Go down any Pinterest rabbit hole, and you'll find hundreds of solutions to make an entryway organized: cubbies, hooks, and shoe racks galore! But for me, it's all about style. When your eye lands on something beautiful, it can trigger a release of dopamine to the brain. Scientists usually point to this phenomenon to describe romantic attraction, but it works in your home too. Create a space that you find truly beautiful, and you'll always feel joy when you walk in the front door. That really gives new meaning to "home is your happy place," doesn't it?

← **A handmade Croft House credenza adds a sophisticated statement to this entryway. Crafted of nearly a hundred individual oak strips and industrial steel casing, it's truly a work of art. A mirror above reflects the shimmering accents of the wall art, bouncing light into the space.**

↑ The ombre wall treatment (hand painted by Bay Area artist Caroline Lizarraga) is calming, which is exactly what interior designer Kristen Peña had in mind. "We wanted the entry wall to almost feel as if you were at the shoreline," she explains. I can't think of anything else that would make me feel more relaxed!

← This is a small space just off of the front door, about 7-feet by 7-feet. "Too tight for any functional space," designer Lada Webster explains. The previous owners had it as a small office—talk about feeling stressed right when you walk in the door! Webster outfitted it with a custom 11-foot bookshelf and a sleek bench to sit and take off your shoes.

When the front door opens right up to the living space, you may be inclined to leave the space bare. However, a few petite picks can help define the space and create a sense of flow from the exterior to the interior. A mirror will reflect light (and allow you to see if you've got lipstick on your teeth before running out the door), while the slim base of the table doesn't take up too much visual real estate; the area still feels open and breezy.

Another angle of this entry by Toronto's Two Fold Interiors reveals a tiled mudroom, complete with a cityscape wallpaper. The playful pattern lets you leave the chaos of the city behind for the comforts of home.

Natural wood adds warmth to this glossy, mid-century foyer, while bold pop art adds a dose of SoCal charm.
(And if you've got an MTV Moon Person, definitely use it as a doorstop. Why not?)

Designer Kate Lester is a pro when it comes to a Modern Coastal vibe. Behind the seagrass-wrapped doors are shelves; each family member can have their own space to put a purse, wallet, keys, or even a pair of grab-and-go shoes.

→ Though this lake house is in Wisconsin, Renee DiSanto of Park and Oak Interior Design says her clients were inspired by the signature style of the East Coast. "In the entry, we started with vertical wood board, ceiling detail, and a stained wood door that gives a warm welcome and sets the tone for the rest of the space," she explains.

↑ "I'm a firm believer in Frank Lloyd Wright's approach to foyers," designer Lauren Svenstrup says. "Going dark and impactful in the entry is a great way to make a first impression, but it also helps to trick the eye to make the rest of the home seem brighter and more open." Here, she used an amazing floral wallpaper with a black background to create that sense of drama, but the colors introduce you to the palette that you'll see throughout the rest of the home.

Open-concept homes can still have a proper entryway moment. A carved table creates division between two spaces and is a great gathering place for keys and other small essentials.

Use what you've got! India Hicks, who lives on Harbour Island in the Bahamas, pays homage to her locale with fresh-cut palm fronds. Though most of us don't live on a tropical island, we can still look to our own yards for inspiration; magnolia or olive branches would also make a great display.

→ While I love this console (it's an old church lectern!), I'm actually most excited about what's behind it. The deep blue railing blends into the wall behind it, so hanging hooks in the stairwell doesn't feel cluttered in the slightest.

↑ A glass stairwell is wrapped in 3M Dichroic Glass Film, which casts colorful shadows in this art-forward Portland home. Designer Stewart Horner of Penny Black Interiors used it to push a few boundaries. "Boundaries are set by dictators," he said in the first issue of *Rue*. "I love to design environments for adventurous, discerning clients."

← Portland designer Donna DuFresne worked with a local artisan to create a custom metal screen for this entry. It physically separates the living area from the front door but still allows ample light through—key in the often-cloudy Pacific Northwest.

↑ Here's an easy upgrade for less than a hundred dollars! You can find unique door knockers at retailers like Pottery Barn, West Elm, or Rejuvenation. For something vintage, flea markets or websites like Chairish and 1st Dibs have a plethora of one-of-a-kind options.

↑ A row of hooks can still be accessorized. I love how a few mementos are leaned against the top, and a frame is hung with some twine. Your purse will look like a piece of art when slung here!

← In this Venice Beach home, by Jette Creative, the front door opens to a wide hallway that leads directly to the kitchen. The ceilings are quite high, so a bench that is tonally similar to the beams helps to ground the room, making the otherwise spare space feel more intimate and welcoming. Two hooks are at the ready for bags, coats, and keys!

Easy Living

Aside from the bedroom, the living room is where we spend the bulk of our time at home. If you're a television and movie fan, it's where you are when Netflix pops in with that pesky question: *Are you still watching?* (Of course I am.) In the winter, enjoying a cup of coffee by the fire on a Saturday morning is the perfect antidote to the busy workweek. It's here that the kids perfect their fort-building skills and the teenagers collapse after a stressful driver's ed test. While formal sitting rooms may not broadcast sporting events, these spaces still serve their purpose well; having a tech-free space in the home has become much more common—a remedy to balance out our hours of screen time. No matter what it looks like, the living room is your unofficial home headquarters; this is the place to feel most comfortable.

One thing I noticed while compiling my favorite living spaces is that no one-size-fits-all formula for the design exists. There's no checklist to follow, where ticking off items will result in a picture-perfect setting. A living room is deeply personal, and everything from the type of sofa you buy to the art you hang on the wall is entirely dependent on your lifestyle and individual tastes. Just as you would when designing a kitchen, start the decorating process by compiling a list of your must-haves. If you spend a lot of time on the sofa, comfort is key and a slim mid-century modern sofa could be an unwise choice for movie marathons. If you love to entertain, make room for a bar cart and maybe a record player. If this is where you do your reading, bring in bookshelves and a great lamp.

In this chapter, you'll see European-inspired sitting rooms alongside uber comfortable family rooms with sectionals that could fit a small army. Which space resonates most with you?

← **You would never guess that a room as elegant as this one would be so family friendly! The microfiber ottoman can easily be wiped clean, while the upholstery of the gray sofa has more than two thread colors. This adds dimension, and the depth of the fabric hides stains better than a flat cotton.**

↓ Though the color palette in this living room is very neutral, interior designer Maayan Kessler brought in an abundance of texture, making this a multi-dimensional design. The fluted finish of the fireplace surround, the nubby upholstery on the sofa and chairs, and even the burl wood side table all bring in interesting visual elements that keep the room from feeling too "black and white."

↑ When choosing throw pillows, it comes down to size and scale. Choose a few different sizes of pillows to nestle together, as designer Tiffany Leigh did here. (If they're all the same size, it will look a bit flat.) For patterns, you want variety: for example, a medium print with organic shapes, an orderly stripe, and a busier plaid all work well together.

← Designer Max Humphrey worked with the architects at Beebe Skidmore to create a comfortable bench that wouldn't obstruct the stunning views of the Pacific Ocean in this Oregon Coast weekend home. They used a durable, fade-resistant outdoor fabric on the cushions to avoid any long-term sun damage. The material also repels stains and is easy to clean, so the homeowners don't need to worry about sandy feet or spills.

↑ The large-scale art could have been centered over the sofa, but the bare wood wall adds much-needed warmth to the sleek, modern room. And though I don't subscribe to the idea of "rules" when it comes to decorating your own home, I do think it's important to design with respect to the home's original style. The clean lines of the mid-century modern architecture are mirrored in the furniture selection (the chairs match the angles of the roof line; the glass tabletop has the same reflective qualities as the tile floor), so each piece looks as if it were made for this house.

↑ A coffee table wrapped in a vintage kilim means no hard corners for little ones to bonk their heads. Trays and books offer a hard surface to set drinks or snacks. A lot of retailers sell similar pieces, but it's an easy DIY. Snag an existing ottoman at Home Goods and recover it with a fabric or rug of your choice. (All you need is a strong staple gun and some good scissors!)

→ To keep your home from looking like a furniture catalog, layer old with new. That's what makes this Manhattan Beach, California, living room by designer Rita Chan feel so welcoming! Vintage pieces sit alongside plush furnishings, which adds warmth and character.

↓ In my opinion, the coolest spaces aren't filled with accessories from big box stores. Just like Mrs. Maisel had a "weird ask," don't shy away from art and objects that are on the funky side—or even plain old weird. If it speaks to you, it has a place in your home.

↑ You don't have to stick to one medium when it comes to art. A blend of photography, illustration, and even framed textiles are what makes this living room so intriguing.

↑ Wood paneling can appear ornate, but this Hollywood Regency library doesn't feel too formal thanks to a neutral sofa and deep-seated armchairs. Laura Muller of Four Point Design Build says well-edited, simple furnishings were intentional here. "Wood breathes so much life into a space, so let it. Keep the lines in the space clean and rhythmic."

↓ For a large sectional, round nesting tables serve as a nice contrast to all the angles, and you can worry less about the dimension and scale of a traditional coffee table. Place the round tables roughly in the center of the room and easily access all areas of the sofa—no bruised shins here.

If you love an all-white, airy space but crave a punch of color, one statement piece (like the ochre velvet sectional here) should do it. Just make sure to bring home a swatch of the fabric before committing to see how the color translates in your space. Natural light is very different from the harsh florescent glow that furniture showrooms are known for.

↑ This formal living space is perfect for parties. The built-in bench at the bay window gives guests a soft place to land, and small drink tables flank the elegant, curved sofa. No guarantees that the light fixture won't beam you up at the end of the night though!

↓ In a larger living space like this one by Laura U Design Collective, a custom serpentine sofa anchors the room. Having seating on both sides connects the large space while offering two different conversation areas.

↑ In this living room by designer Montana Labelle, window coverings go all the way up the wall, which tricks the eye into thinking the ceiling is higher than it is. This white linen ripple-fold curtain is on a recessed drapery track invisible to the eye.

→ The reality is that most of us use our living spaces to watch television. (And with so many epic shows available at the click of a button, who could blame us?) It's always been a big trend to camouflage the TV, which is a fantastic solution if you're rarely using the remote. If you never miss an episode, don't go through the trouble of hiding it! This white oak TV surround looks like art in itself.

↑ Why "knot" go bold in the living room? Studio Munroe paired stripes with the coolest poufs (from Knots Studio) in this San Francisco condo. The lightweight pieces are funky and versatile—use them as meditation pillows or extra seating for game nights.

↓ Variety is the spice of life, especially on these floating shelves. The key to looking cool and not chaotic? Focus on complementary colors, shapes, and sizes. Create a foundation with books first. You'll see some are stacked and organized by color, while others with interesting covers face forward like a piece of art. A blend of vintage finds are mixed in—start with the largest pieces first, placing them evenly so the look is balanced, and then layer in smaller treasures. You want the eye to travel! Every time I visit this living room, I discover something new.

↑ I love the look of a marble coffee table, but if you're using it regularly—for drinks, flowers, or candles—you'll want to protect it. A few chic coasters or trays will keep the marble from staining.

← The easiest way to add architectural interest to a room is with contrasting trim. There's nothing basic about this room, where white millwork stands out against a moody green and gray palette.

← This gallery wall by reDesign Home utilizes different framing materials (gilt wood, black wood, raw wood), and some of the art is even unframed. The variety implies the art was collected over time.

→ Closed cabinets at the base of this shelving unit hide all the living room must-haves, like remotes, extra blankets, or toys. To add dimension, an unframed painting is mounted on the shelf's exterior. Hanging or leaning the art against the wall is the expected placement, so while this is an unusual choice, it's out of the box (literally!) and quite striking. It also allows for taller items on the shelves while keeping the art on full display.

↑ If you don't have space for a bookshelf, a tiered table can be used for easily accessed storage.
It looks clever, not cluttered.

← When in doubt, go custom! If you're on the hunt for a perfect piece, a local woodworker can bring your
vision to life. When designer Gabrielle Aker realized most record stands were mid-century, she worked
with her husband's company, Aker Studios, to create something more organic that would work as a bar
and a bookshelf and keep the tunes going all night.

↑　If you want to get people on the internet riled up, post a picture with the spines of books facing inward. (It's almost as bad as posting something political or disclosing that you've never seen *Lord of the Rings*.) I say, as long as there are books, and they're arranged in a way that makes you happy, that's all that matters.

→　If you prefer an orderly space, even numbers are your friend: two matching chairs, two matching sofas, four matching light fixtures. Though symmetry in interior design can feel a bit safe, the wiry light fixtures here are anything but monotonous.

↑ To highlight the architectural elements of this cabin, the same dark paint coats the walls, window frames, and beams. It offers a strong contrast to the snowy scene outside.

← For busy families, trays on the coffee table keep everything neatly confined. Don't feel as if you need to get rid of all your stuff to have a well-styled space; it's more about finding clever styling hacks. Here you'll also see a small basket off to the side that stores dog toys.

↑ To add depth and dimension, the interior of these shelves was painted a glossy green. It's a perfect canvas for the homeowner's eclectic collection.

↑ For a lot of color and pattern, allow the main pieces to be fairly neutral. A creamy Cisco Home sofa lets this vintage rug take center stage. As for the rug's size, just make sure it's large enough for the front legs of the furniture to land on top of it. This helps define the space.

↑ Built-in benches flank either side of this striking marble fireplace, offering extra seating without cutting into the square footage of the room. I really love seeing the natural wood grain alongside the slight veining of the black stone.

↑ I call this an "open-ish" floor plan. Floor-to-ceiling steel rods separate the kitchen, stairwell, and den but allow light to travel through all three spaces. Plus, the shelves feel like a mini art installation. They're just the right size for a few plants, books, and framed art.

Pull up a Chair

My husband and I recently bought our first house. Like all moves, it started out totally chaotic—until we got a small tulip table and two chairs set up in my new kitchen's breakfast nook. With a place to sit and eat lunch in between unpacking boxes, my husband and I found stability. I'd be lying if I said I didn't immediately start dreaming how we could put a built-in banquette along the corner and upgrade the light fixture to something more our style, but we still had that comforting feeling that we were finally beginning the new chapter we had long imagined. And even when the unpacking took way longer than anticipated, as it always does, the daily routine of gathering at the table made our new house feel like home.

As I look back on memories of past homes, most of the noteworthy moments happened around the dinner table or saddled up to the kitchen counter. The dining table in my childhood home hosted holiday dinners and, with newspaper protecting the wood, was a great place for my brother to paint model airplanes and cars while I played with my paper dolls. In college, my friends and I gathered around our hand-me-down tables, eating cheap pizza, studying for finals, and laughing at the weekend's events. My apartment in San Francisco was the setting for my first Thanksgiving away from family, and it was where I learned that you need to buy groceries long before the Macy's Parade begins. That morning we discovered our local market had sold out of turkey, ham, and even rotisserie chicken! We grabbed a few slices of deli meat, and it became one of my most memorable meals, enjoyed by candlelight in the bay window of our dining room.

Needless to say, the dining table is where life happens.

← Family-friendly yet elegant, designer Katie Hodges' work shows us it's possible. Constructed with unsealed salvaged wood, which intentionally shows imperfections like nicks, nail holes, and knots, this farm-style table has an antiqued, time-worn quality from the start (a spill will only add to its character), while the chairs can be easily wiped down.

↑ Built-in banquettes are genius. Not only can the whole family pile in and hang out, but the base can also store that Instant Pot or air fryer you promised yourself you'd use!

← To make the most of this dining space, design duo Mister + Mrs Sharp created a wall-to-wall banquette in a friendly blue hue. "With chairs, we can easily gather around the table for a dinner party of eight, but for larger, more casual gatherings, many more can be accommodated," they explain.

↑ This is a fabulous small space solution and one that will get a lot of use—breakfast and homework both go great here. A round table (whether an iconic marble Saarinen or IKEA's budget-friendly version), a chair or two, and a solitary fixture are key.

→ For a family-friendly banquette, a stain-repellent upholstery is key. Try performance fabrics for easy clean up. (Crypton and Sunbrella have beautiful options.) Bonus points if the chosen fabric is patterned— the busyness will act as a camouflage for stains.

↓ If your space has odd angles, a round table will fit nicely in the room—you don't have to worry as much about the table's placement or lining it up with the wall. The three prongs of the light fixture ensure even lighting for all guests (or for doing puzzles).

← Here the lines of the light fixture run parallel to the lines of the windows, which complements the room's architecture instead of competing with it.

If you've fallen in love with a fixture, but it's too small for the space, double up! Here, two artful pendant lamps, originally designed by Mario Bellini for Artemide in 1974, offer ample lighting and a dose of symmetry.

↑ If you don't have a separate dining space, try out a small round table in the living room. It works as a charming spot for a leisurely Sunday brunch or for working on a puzzle.

→ I grew up with a similar antique buffet in my family's dining room. It stored all of my mother's fancy platters and table linens. If you love to entertain (and are blessed with a formal dining room), this is a must.

The buffet and dining chairs are in line with this home's Spanish Revival architecture, but the table and light fixture add a bit of modern glam. It's important to honor a home's style, but mixing in pieces you love, even if they're a departure from the architectural style, is the key to making it your own.

↓ I don't think there's anything more charming than a dining nook. Since this space is rectangular, it might seem intuitive to match the angles with a rectangular table. A tulip table and a circular rug actually allow for more movement in and out of the space. Wouldn't this be a fun spot for late-night board games? And A+ for the upholstered, cushioned chairs. Comfort is key when the backgammon competition is fierce!

↑ A pony wall, a wall that comes only halfway up normal wall height and is adorably named after the shorter walls added to stables for ponies, divides the kitchen and dining area here. It offers a more formal place to eat, but guests can still be part of the action.

↑ No, this red room is not a nod to Christian Grey, but bringing the color all the way up and across the ceiling does feel romantic. Paint is always a great way to get a luxe look for less.

← If the electrical box isn't centered over the table, a fluid light fixture like this one is ideal. You don't need any major electrical work for it to be centered to your table.

↑ So, how low should a chandelier go? It all depends on the light fixture itself. If it's petite and squarely centered over the table, it can land roughly 30 to 36 inches above the tabletop. If it's leggy, like this one, and runs the risk of taking an eye out, higher is better. Your tall friends will thank you.

→ Instead of the ubiquitous oversize kitchen island, try something new! Two Fold Interiors opted for a slender island and a long and narrow table that can accommodate the entire family.

↑ Inspired by her favorite pattern (Queen of Spain from Schumacher), designer Lauren Svenstrup broke out the paint. She hand-stamped each droplet for a one-of-a-kind wall treatment.

→ Dining room art should serve as a conversation starter. Here, designer India Hicks lined her walls with framed maps, featuring stories of past adventures.

↑ I love a faux architectural moment! An arched mirror adds interest to a boxy new-build, designed by Two / Tone Interiors. If arches aren't your thing, a large windowpane mirror (about the same length as the table) could achieve a similar effect.

← A long console in the dining room is a great spot to display art, vases, and other favorite accessories, and it can easily be cleared to make way for larger holiday meals. A note on lighting: next time you're at your favorite restaurant, keep an eye on how the owners have lit the place. A variety of sources (overhead, sconces, and lamps) is not only flattering, but it casts a more romantic glow.

↑ Though dining room sets are a thing of the past, they still work well in homes that look historic. If you've inherited one, play up the vintage charm, as designer Sarah Birnie did here, with textured wallpaper, ornate light fixtures, and art that would have come from the same time frame.

→ Slim bookshelves (you can snag similar ones from IKEA) hold dozens of India Hicks's family photos. The majority of the photos are printed in black and white—making the collection feel less like a family album and more like a work of art. (Though not all of us are lucky enough to call the royal family, well, family. Look closely, and you might see some familiar faces. India is the goddaughter of Prince Charles and was a bridesmaid in Princess Diana's wedding!)

↑ This old farm table is surrounded by sleek, modern chairs from Design Within Reach (it's called the Nerd Chair). It's not necessarily an unexpected choice—great design is all about mixing genres—but the decision to add in one oak chair among the mostly black set is one thing that makes this Novogratz-designed space memorable.

← Though the table is fairly traditional, the rest of this setup embodies the Wild West. The rope on the light fixture looks as if it was plucked from a cool old saloon, and the mix-and-match chairs have a great rustic quality as well. If you're drawn to the nostalgic charm of the Old West, pick one or two design elements to add to your space for the most impact. If you add more, there is the risk of being too "on the nose" or looking like a movie set.

The New Bar and Restaurant

I have no shame in admitting I didn't really learn to cook until Los Angeles issued shelter-in-place orders in March 2020 and my favorite restaurants were forced to close their doors. I'm exaggerating a bit—I could certainly make a few key dishes—but I was not at all proficient in the kitchen. With each passing week, however, I became more confident in my ability to make something I would enjoy eating. (And let me tell you, perfecting deep-dish pizza was a real highlight of quarantine.)

As my skills sharpened, so did my opinions on what makes a great kitchen. We spend so much time analyzing countertop choices, the look of the appliances, the hardware and plumbing fixtures. But we need to look beyond aesthetics! A pretty Instagram snap of a sunny kitchen might not disclose "there is not actually a spot to efficiently store cutting boards" or "the open shelving means I keep my single-use appliances in the linen closet."

I mention this to say, take these design ideas with a grain of salt. What works beautifully in one home might not provide enough room for your sourdough breadmaking. If you regularly cook with foods that are high in acidity or enjoy making craft cocktails, be mindful of what countertops you choose: natural stone will stain and tarnish really quickly with exposure to vinegar, citrus, and alcohol. If you love to fry and sear on the stovetop, the exhaust hood should be top priority.

If you're more like Carrie Bradshaw of *Sex and the City,* no worries, as your stove will simply store your sweaters. But for the rest of us, really focus on how your kitchen will best function for your household's needs. Then choose all the finishing touches and special details to really make it yours.

← Creating a black kitchen takes some guts, but this photo of the outcome is one of our most-shared Instagram posts. Chicago design firm Studio Sven dubbed it Castle Black, referencing *Game of Thrones* and Lauren Svenstrup's favorite color palette. It's edgy and sophisticated, and a mix of matte and shiny surfaces gives the room plenty of dimension.

Open shelving is a current trend in kitchens, but if you have a lot of storage needs, then this may not be the most practical choice for you. Keep cabinets for the bulk of the space, and use only a few floating shelves to display your favorite pieces and beautifully-packaged cooking staples.

↑ Open shelving isn't just for the walls. Here, a few extra inches of cabinet space resulted in stylish storage for well-loved cookbooks.

→ The backsplash in this Toronto kitchen by designer Ashley Montgomery is faux brick, which subtly plays up the English-country vibe. Also, I'm a big fan of art in the kitchen—it's a way to show your personality beyond utilitarian items like cutting boards and appliances. One caution: For kitchen art, choose something inexpensive from a thrift store so you don't have to worry about sauces or oils damaging it.

↓ Free up a cupboard! In this Los Angeles kitchen, a curtain rod and S-hooks hold pots, pans, and colanders above the window while still allowing light in.

→ This large island not only has room for two, its open shelves house cookbooks, placemats, and a beloved teapot collection.

↑ Though it looks high-end, this kitchen is actually affordable IKEA. The designers swapped out the doors for a custom option and built all of the appliances into the cabinets.

← You don't have to do a backsplash the entire length of the wall. Hive LA Home put a geometric tile just behind the range to catch any spills, offering just the right amount of color to the otherwise-neutral space.

↑ Follow Kristen Peña's lead and think outside of the box when it comes to counter stools! This red pair adds a dose of personality to an otherwise simple space.

→ If you have your heart set on a designer item, but your budget is tapped, look to sample sales! If you can't find a full set, mix and match chairs with the same shape and different finishes for a cohesive-yet-funky vibe.

You can mix materials in
your kitchen as designer
Rita Chan did here. Stone is
used as the backsplash by
the stove, while patterned
tile on the right designates
the coffee bar. In the
middle, an oak island and
leather chairs stray from
the all-white palette,
adding dimension and an
organic, earthy quality.

↑ To lighten the visual load in this open-concept kitchen, there are no upper cabinets. To make up for the loss of storage, open shelving was added to the island. And because the dishes are all black, they feel like a collection versus a necessity.

↓ A thin iron rod adds height and industrial charm to these shelves, but more importantly, it keeps everything from toppling over. This is handy if you live in earthquake-prone California, but is great for anyone wanting to display taller items.

↑ This island is massive. To keep it from feeling too visually heavy, Alessia Zanchi Loffredo and Sarah Coscarelli of reDesign Home designed it with legs so that it sits raised above the floor.

→ The at-home happy hour just leveled up. If your home has a butler's pantry in the floor plan, why not convert it to a bar? The glass-front cabinets can display your glassware and favorite spirits. Choose a durable stone for the countertop; citrus and alcohol can stain marble and other porous surfaces.

White kitchens are nearly as controversial as books facing backward. Some people love them; some people love to hate them. This one by interior designer Katie Hodges is done right though! The massive pendants make a major style statement, while the slate gray of the island is grounding and the natural wood stools add an organic pop.

This show-stopper kitchen by Toronto designer Maayan Kessler has a lot of wonderful details to soak up. Peek at the upper cabinets— fluted glass doors disguise the contents but still feel open. It's a charming look and a nice compromise if you want open shelving but don't want the pressure of keeping things "styled" all the time.

↑ Retractable doors can hide appliances and other items that you use every day but don't necessarily want to *see* every day.

→ Fresh herbs in terracotta pots look beautiful. If your grocery store has those hydroponically grown living herbs, drop the plastic container directly into a chic vessel. No green thumb required.

Instead of choosing wood for your open shelving, use stone for an extra "wow" moment. These marble shelves match the countertops and backsplash, visually leading the eye upward, and the light fixture feels almost like a beautiful bowl, styled right alongside the other ceramics. If you're on a tight budget, visit a local slab yard to source some remnant stone. A piece of marble with a depth of ten inches and about two feet long should be plenty, and it doesn't necessarily have to match your backsplash to a T.

"We wanted it to be modern, but since the home is right on the beach and mountains, we wanted to incorporate earth tones to bring the outside in," designer Genna Margolis shares. "We wanted the finishes to be simple but special, which is why we went with a glazed terracotta brick tile for the backsplash," she says. She coated the cabinets in a greige paint, to keep them from looking too basic, and added walnut floating shelves.

↓ It's often one or two pieces that can elicit the most dramatic change. Glossy black pendant lights and Bend Goods counter stools give this all-white, builder-grade kitchen a subtle mod vibe.

→ Remove the black paint above the cabinets, and this kitchen becomes less interesting. Inspires you to think outside the box in your own space, doesn't it?

↑ A linear light fixture echoes the lines of the kitchen, only highlighting the view. To keep the space functional, a long shelf stretches the length of the window with just enough space for a few cookbooks and plants.

↑ Designer Montana Labelle scored mid-century travertine "that had been sitting around" before the kitchen design started. "We actually used the backside of it, which we thought was more interesting," she says.

↑ Styling a kitchen can go further than a few cutting boards leaned against the wall. Small hooks hold functional pieces, like the colander, as well as some art. Here the driftwood balances out the black countertops.

↑ When in Rome, or in this case, Joshua Tree . . . why not saddle up to the counter for a stack of flapjacks? This kitchen is fun, it's funky, it's not for everyone—and that's exactly the point.

→ A minty green pendant plays off of the island's blue hue in this space designed by Clara Jung of Banner Day Interiors. There was no construction necessary to create the breakfast nook: a thin bench fits perfectly along the wall here.

↑ "The original kitchen was not wide enough for a traditional island, so we opted for an antique French rectory table," designer Amy Sklar says of this historic Pasadena home. If you don't need the extra storage, this will give your kitchen that extra design oomph. If storage is crucial, IKEA has some pieces that are just as petite, but offer shelving and drawers.

↑ Kitchen styling is usually focused on functional pieces, like utensils or ceramic serving dishes. I say: don't forget the art! This contemporary collection is really cool and infuses the kitchen with the homeowner's personality.

↓ Though this home is in a coastal community, the owners wanted to pull inspiration from their time spent in London. Pale purple light fixtures and brass legs on the island would be right at home in Notting Hill.

The kitchen and dining room here would each be beautiful on their own, but they also work harmoniously together. Designer Kristen Peña relied on a similar color palette for both spaces, as well as complementary shapes. (Notice how the dining chairs and kitchen stools are different in style, but each have a similar curved back?) Peña ensured the space would feel cohesive from top to bottom by using only black accents.

Rest and Relaxation

Each day begins and ends in the same place: the bedroom. This space can affect your entire day, for better or worse. I had the realization a few years ago—when laundry was piled up on the chair in the corner and my laptop was perched on my nightstand—that I was setting myself up for extra stress. When "tasks" are the last thing you see before drifting off to sleep and the first thing you see when you open your eyes, you never really feel that sense of accomplishment. The bedroom should be relaxing, and the decor you bring into the space can deeply influence how rested you feel.

Did you know that a beautiful, tidy bedroom actually can affect our mental health? When I was a moody teenager, my mom got on my case every single morning, insisting that I needed to make my bed. I'd chirp back, "Why would I make it if I'm just going to ruin it again in a few hours?" Much to my chagrin, she was right. Studies show that making the bed each day can spark joy, improve productivity, and lower stress. By kickstarting your day with this simple chore, you'll feel accomplished and in control, which in turn can encourage a more-structured routine. A clutter-free space leads to a clutter-free mind. Yep. Turns out making the bed is a bit of a mind game.

When designing a bedroom, think about the elements of your favorite hotel room. There is a comfortable mattress, cozy bedding, and window coverings that block out everything. If you're like me and love to stay in bed late on the weekends, multiple types of window coverings are a key; just as in a hotel, you can have blackout shades for your most restful sleep and sheer panels to create a bit of ethereal ambiance.

This room should be grounding, allowing you to fully reconnect with yourself and completely recharge.

← To maximize the ocean views beyond the sliding barn doors, designer Max Humphrey chose to "float" this bed in the center of the room. "Logistically I would have put the bed on the wall adjacent to the bathroom, where it would fit, but then you're waking up and looking at a wall instead of waking up and looking at the ocean," he says. Behind, there's a slim console table with plenty of convenient plugs.

Though it's not the tidiest option, pooling the linens at the base of the bed is a fashion-forward way to "make the bed." Plus, it's a lot easier than folding hospital corners each morning! Here, to avoid looking sloppy, the window coverings barely kiss the floor.

Using an iconic teak and cane V-leg armchair, originally designed by Swiss architect Pierre Jeanneret in the 1950s, as a nightstand is an unexpected choice. But it's a great solution if you're like me and can't stop collecting chairs. And as a nightstand, the chair offers just enough room for a few books and a stylish catchall to keep jewelry.

No room for a nightstand? Mount everything to the wall! A small box offers a tabletop and room for books, while the light offers a lovely glow.

↑ "We wanted a little more whimsy," designer Kristen Peña explains. "So, we chose a hand-painted wallpaper by Porter Teleo. But we didn't want it to be a whole, full room of wallpaper. We added millwork to treat it as a wainscot, so that the wallpaper almost feels like it's an extension of the headboard."

← This bedroom is composed of similar neutral shades, so it feels as if you're sleeping in a cloud.

↑ A bedroom can be a bit more adventurous when it comes to accessorizing. I love that the vintage helmet feels like a nod to a teenager's bedroom, despite it being designed by Studio Munroe for a busy professional living in a San Francisco high-rise.

↓ Is there anything better than a great hotel room? To recreate that vibe at home, you've got to pull from the hotel's playbook: sheer drapes and blackout shades are key. Everhem is a great resource for custom window coverings.

↑ In a snug space, explore lighting options like this. Hung from the ceiling, these bug-like fixtures offer just the right amount of reading light without needing to take up precious space on the nightstand.

↑ If the only place for the bed is against the window, a thick drapery behind can act as a headboard. Just ensure that there's enough space between the bed and the window to easily open and close the coverings.

If you're in a rental and can't do a thing about your bedroom's carpeting, it's no biggie. A small scatter rug at your bedside achieves the same look as a full-size rug and gives your feet a plush landing pad each morning. If you want to make other changes to your rental, like painting a room or swapping out light fixtures, show your landlords an inspiration image! If your landlords can see your vision, they're more likely to green light the changes.

A four-poster bed feels regal, and I think this framed lady would agree. Also, the secret to getting your pillows to look like a hotel bed? That bolster behind keeps everything propped up neatly.

← You can fake millwork with paint or wallpaper. It's far more cost effective than installing molding, not to mention quicker. It's a great option if you're in a rental and can't permanently alter the space.

↑ You don't necessarily need a headboard. A large textile mounted to the wall will provide the same look—just make sure it's at least as wide as the mattress. Here, a Moroccan wedding blanket adds texture and symmetry to the space.

↑ We often see benches at the end of the bed, but what about a desk? This makes the most of a small space and is a great idea if you live with roommates and have only one room that's all your own. If you have to hop on a Zoom call, no one will know you're in the bedroom!

← To up the cozy ante, a variety of vintage rugs can be patchworked together. Danny Seo layered rugs here in his Pennsylvania home, but if it's a high traffic area, you can take your rugs to a local upholstery shop to be stitched together for a totally custom piece.

Though the bright white walls (and camera angle) make this bedroom appear quite airy, it's a snug space. Maximize nightstand real estate by using a swing-arm sconce attached to the wall instead of a table lamp. If you look closely, these are plug-ins, so no need for an electrician!

A hanging headboard is a great solution if you're short on space. There are a lot of chic options at all price points. If you're crafty, it's a project that wouldn't be too tough to DIY: A towel rack and a few slim cushions can be fastened to the wall for added comfort.

↓ Black Porter Teleo wallpaper wraps this San Francisco bedroom, while a custom headboard spans the length of the wall. Gold details, from the sconces to the window frame, play off the paper's metallic accents.

← Ever wonder what type of bedding you should order? To be honest, *Rue* could probably publish a trilogy on the matter. The most common sheets on the market are percale, sateen, linen, and brushed cotton . . . and at the end of the day, it comes down to personal preference. In short: Percale is cool to the touch with a matte finish. Sateen is buttery soft and has a slight sheen. Linen is light and airy and often has an effortless (aka slightly wrinkled) look. Brushed cotton has the softest pile, almost like your favorite T-shirt.

The Loo

A bathroom is the best place in the house for a design risk. You can push the boundaries with your material choices here, going for bold and bright or choosing a neutral wall finish that will feel like a luxury spa. However, bathrooms also are definitely the room in the house where there are admittedly more "rules" to follow.

If you're embarking on a renovation, you've likely saved up dozens of inspiration photos, but don't forget the basics. Consider how much moisture will be in the space before committing to wallpaper. If the room stays excessively steamy, the paper will bubble and peel right off. A less glamorous piece of advice is to make sure that the toilet paper roll is within easy reach and that you won't hit your knees when you sit down. Really take stock of your storage needs before ripping out a medicine cabinet or vanity with extra drawers. Though an elegant sconce is a beautiful option, will it provide the best lighting as you do your makeup? Is the electrical outlet in a convenient place for your hair dryer?

Needless to say, don't let the quick transformations you see on home renovation shows inspire you to break out the sledgehammer without doing some solid research. To avoid costly mistakes, speak to your contractor and plumber thoroughly before committing to any design plans.

Now that I'm off my soapbox, I can't reiterate enough to go wild! Don't be limited by builder-grade finishes, but choose materials in a color you truly love. Let your sense of humor shine with funky art, or design an all-neutral space that allows you to just turn your brain off during a long soak in the tub. Your bathroom can be the ultimate self-care oasis.

← This is one of the most popular rooms we've ever shared. The homeowners are quite lucky to have a massive bathroom, but designer Erin Chelius didn't want it to feel too cold or empty. Though the tub is the star, the details you should notice are the different geometric tiles, which break up the space, and the white oak vanity, which adds warmth.

→ Zellige tile is a great option if you want a dark and moody bathroom. Its reflective qualities will help natural light dance throughout the room.

↑ A statement floating sink highlights the Bordeaux tone in the Calacatta Viola marble. To make the marble pop even more, Aker Interiors painted this small powder bathroom with Portola Paints Roman Clay in Black Star. It's an eco-friendly plaster finish and is easy for even the most DIY-adverse to use.

To save space in a petite bathroom, plumbing should be wall-mounted. If you're like me and prefer things always clean and tidy, you'll want a small squeegee at the ready to keep the flat basin pristine between deep cleans. (Beard trimmings won't stand a chance.)

If your home has hardwood throughout, you can still have that showstopping tile moment. Just take it up the wall, as designer Kate Lester did here in Manhattan Beach, California.

↑ This hexagonal marble tile on the wall is usually reserved for floors, but I love how it balances the bold pattern on these floor tiles. You can typically find similar tile at Home Depot or Lowe's, and it's priced well, making it a cost-efficient choice for a larger surface area.

→ If you're worried about a bold tile being "too much," keep all of the other elements simple. White subway tile is functional on the walls and allows the statement to stay on the floor.

↑ What I love most about these concrete sinks by Nood is that they come in fourteen different color options. Here, a peachy pastel looks cheerful alongside terrazzo floors. (Fun fact! This image was the cover of our very last digital magazine, which we released right at the start of the pandemic. A not-so-subtle reminder for readers to wash their hands!)

← Think outside the builder-grade bathroom vanity! If you find a piece you love at a flea market or garage sale, be it an old dresser or a sturdy table, a local plumber can help you retrofit it with a sink.

↓ When working with different types of tile, they should be similar, but different. The colors should be complementary, but the scale is key—the small pattern isn't competing with the burgundy subway tile or the hexagonal floor beyond.

← Black limestone tile, installed in a herringbone pattern, adds a lot of depth to this primary bath. The black window frame and light fixture add balance, ensuring the floor doesn't feel too visually heavy.

→ Micro-cement, a resin and cement mixture, applied thinly to walls, is the secret behind this chic bath. It even wraps a standard tub to look like pricey marble. It takes careful application—if you're not into DIYs, leave this one to the professionals—but is far less expensive than traditional stone wraps.

↑ Though unlacquered brass is a popular choice for plumbing fixtures, polished nickel, on both the faucet and the light fixtures, adds a timeless element to this black-and-white bath by JDP Interiors. Wallpaper by L'Aviva Home was custom printed to fit the dimensions of the room perfectly.

↑ Good things come in small packages! Calacatta marble wraps the custom sink, and a mirror spans the wall with a sconce installed just to the side, making the most of every inch of the room.

→ The same marble was used both on the vanity and the shower wall, the beauty of which is caught in the mirror here. These carefully planned moments can make a space.

Lighting is much less important in a powder room since it's not the space you shower or get ready in. Installing the light fixture off center adds character and won't affect your makeup routine.

Even if you don't have room for a seated vanity, you can still channel a bit of the same Hollywood glamour. Display your prettiest beauty products and use a vintage silver cup for makeup brushes. Your most-used items will look like art.

Unless you want to give your neighbors a show, most bathrooms require window coverings. Call a local seamstress to check into creating something custom using a durable (and water resistant!) outdoor fabric.

Floor-to-ceiling sheer drapes provide privacy without blocking natural light or the view beyond.

↑ The powder room is the perfect place to use a bold wallpaper; I love A-Street Prints, Chasing Paper, and Mitchell Black for wallpaper and wall murals. Not only will the smaller space ensure that the pattern doesn't feel like "too much," but these spaces are also low-risk for moisture damage.

← With careful planning, a powder room makeover could happen in a weekend! The original pedestal sink still stands, but a soft patterned wallpaper, brass plumbing fixtures, a new light, and a large mirror give the space a fresh look.

They say that design is in the details, and it couldn't be truer in this bathroom that's been outfitted in Ann Sacks tile. At the base, blue tile was carefully installed horizontally, while the softer green is laid vertically. A closer look reveals that all of the grout lines match up perfectly—a detail you might not even notice unless it had been installed incorrectly. If you're designing a bathroom yourself, provide your contractor with detailed drawings and instructions to make sure your vision is executed perfectly.

A wooden cart is nestled in the corner, storing extra towels and displaying a vintage art piece and lamp. While it's not the lighting source you'd use for getting ready, it casts a relaxing glow while in the tub.

↑ Leaf-printed wallpaper by Cole & Son adds a touch of whimsy to this bathroom by designer Clara Jung. The tile flooring is an affordable option that will look classic for many years.

← In this powder room by Studio Munroe, a Duravit corner sink allows for maximum viewing of the wall covering—Christian Lacroix's Bois Paradis Bourgeon. It's a work of art!

The Rumpus Room

Though I'm not a mom yet, I've written about hundreds of children's spaces over the years. One thing that always sort of bothered me, however, was this narrative that you should design for your kids in a way that won't disrupt your own aesthetic. As a design lover (and someone who is generally averse to bright colors), I can certainly respect this, but it feels a bit backward. When creating a space for children, the top priority should be that they feel loved, safe, and important.

Designing for a child calls for considering a few key elements, and age is at the top of the list. For babies, a convertible crib that can grow with them from the newborn stage to the toddler years is central. Older kids will need a desk for schoolwork, as well as a great organizational system that they can easily access to keep everything corralled but within reach.

Luckily, paying attention to such key considerations doesn't mean kids' rooms have to look like a toy store. You can create a beautiful, colorful, and creative space modeled after your children's interests. You can use color in an impactful way and pull in eclectic pieces that will foster their imaginations. You can prioritize reading and playing and learning. You can use cozy textiles to make children feel comfy and soft furnishings to make sure they don't get hurt reenacting the dance off in *Trolls: World Tour*. Most importantly, you can choose durable pieces that are easy to clean, so they feel free to let their creativity soar and make the occasional mess. Finally, once your little ones are old enough to express an opinion, let them weigh in on the design! Choosing their own decor is a wonderful way to help them express their identities.

← Flat-weave rugs are super durable and easy to clean—a great choice for an active tween. If there are spills, just blot up excess moisture with a paper towel, and a tiny bit of soap and water should handle the rest.

Designer Jenn Feldman used shelving for books and sporting equipment. This keeps everything off the floor and ends up looking like a colorful art installation.

Instead of shelves, cute army-inspired pockets are a great solution for books.

If you're on the fence with the color kids have chosen to decorate their room, a great compromise is to go halfsies. Literally! Take the color only halfway up the wall. It will look great and won't overpower the space.

← The wallpaper is statement enough, so all-white furniture tones it down a bit. "The mini Eames-inspired kids' set is cute and simple and a nod to good design, which is sometimes hard to find in kids' furniture," designer Sandra Fox says.

↑ Growing up with a trundle bed was the highlight of my childhood—so many slumber parties! Mine wasn't quite this cool, though. Cortney Novogratz wrapped these IKEA beds in a beautiful Jonathan Adler for Kravet fabric to make them more sophisticated.

→ Powder-coated white desks are so easy to clean. A wet wipe should get most of the mess, and a magic eraser can tackle permanent marker mistakes.

↑ With many students opting for remote learning, a desk in the bedroom has become a necessity. Placing it in front of the window will inspire creativity, and since it's facing away from the bed, kids won't feel like they're trapped in the same room all day.

↑ A built-in bench is the perfect spot for kids to tackle their summer reading list. Drawers below offer toy storage; they can dump everything in them at the end of the day.

→ Choose a piece of art that will remind your young teens that they can change the world. A soft leather ottoman in place of a coffee table will keep emergency room visits to a minimum for days when the sofa is a launch pad.

↑ A playful tile will make bath time more fun. The bright blue complements the floral wallpaper in the adjacent room.

→ Any spot that inspires more reading is a very good thing. A daybed or cozy chair that is just for the kids gives a sense of ownership and will encourage them to curl up with a good book instead of asking for more screen time. When creating a gallery wall, let your kids weigh in on the pieces you hang. They'll be drawn to art that expresses their personalities and be proud to hang out in the space.

→ In this game room by the Novogratz, the yellow sofa is actually a futon from their eponymous furniture line. Great for last-minute sleepovers!

↓ Imagination is key in early childhood and plays a big role in creative development. An aviary-inspired wallpaper on the ceiling will spark imagination. The whimsical pattern might lead to many a game of make-believe and offers a fun view for any little eyes peeking out of an elaborate sofa-cushion fort.

Displaying a kiddo's beloved collection will bring a sense of pride to their space. Here, a row of Funko Pop! toys stand guard over the bed.

↑ Any new parent will tell you that window treatments are one of the most important elements in a nursery! Blackout shades literally block out all the light from a room, and some are even crafted with additional lining to muffle exterior noise. You can work with a designer to create something custom or look to online retailers like Everhem to create something bespoke for your space.

→ I have a soft spot for pink wallpaper in little girls' rooms. (Growing up, I had a pink carousel scene, and I found it mesmerizing.) Here, though, my focus is on the custom shelving the designer installed alongside the window seat. It's such a smart design to maximize storage space.

Something Extra

Every home has those spaces that feel like a big question mark. In my last home, it was this too-small bedroom right off the dining room. It wasn't quite large enough for a guest bed. There was no natural light, so I didn't fancy using it for my home office. There was an attached bathroom, which we used for guests, and so the center of the space needed to be clear for foot traffic. We shoved the cat's litter box in the corner and, slowly but surely, it became the room where junk started to accumulate. I wish I had thoughtfully taken the time to address the needs of my house and use it to create a functional, beautiful space. In hindsight, built-in storage along one wall would have held cleaning supplies tucked away neatly and kept the litter box out of sight. Learn from my mistakes! Make the most of your home, even those weird little rooms.

In this chapter, I want to highlight those less-frequented spaces that might feel a little odd or require extra creativity to reach their peak potential. I'm endlessly inspired by the interior designers who see these anomalous spaces and immediately envision how to breathe new life into them. There's a home bar that feels so fabulously old Hollywood, a room that's gone to the dogs, and functional home offices in unexpected corners. Putting fresh eyes on these unused nooks can transform them into your favorite room in the house.

← California designer Linda Hayslett turned a storage space under the stairs into a clever and cozy spot for Remington, her client's cute corgi. A small dog bed can be pulled out easily for cleaning, and toys can be out of sight in a basket behind that wall.

↑ Instead of opting for extra storage, designer Emilie Munroe outfitted this nook with a plaid wallcovering and colorful glass light fixture. The loveseat fits snuggly inside, making this a great spot to take off your shoes or for the kids to curl up with a book.

← A hallway is never just a hallway. It's an opportunity to make a major statement. This Hollywood home features a mirrored sign found at a local flea market. Not only does it reflect light—making the space feel larger—and offer a spot for a last-minute lipstick check, but it's also super cool.

↑ Behold, the power of built-ins! Instead of finding chairs or a bench that fit the space, Park and Oak Interior Design fitted the nook with a charming window seat. The ticking stripe of the bench cushion is smaller in scale than the plaid on the Roman shade, so they complement each other nicely. If you create something similar, don't forget to add hinges to the top of the bench so you can open and close it—you can store extra linens or games inside.

→ A shopping hack I love? Look to retailers that cater to kids and teens for unexpected furniture finds. This sofa and ottoman are from RH Teen. The set would look amazing in a playroom, but when styled with a vintage rug and linen pillows, it's decidedly grown up.

↑   Forgoing one lower cabinet for a built-in dog bed is one of the best ideas ever, especially for curious pups who are always on your heels while you're cooking. They can have their own safe space, and you won't have to worry about constantly shooing them out of the kitchen.

←   A bedroom for just dogs? "Every project brings something new to the table, but this was definitely a first," designer Jennifer Vaquero laughs. An on-the-nose wallpaper adds charm, while other elements were chosen for durability and cleanability. The rug is FLOR tiles, so you can swap one out if the mess is too far gone.

→ This room was previously an empty landing at the top of the stairs, but reDesign Home made it the ultimate family hangout. To bring down the scale of the space and make it feel cozier, wood beams were added to the gabled ceiling.

↓ A basement or den is the perfect place to push the boundaries. Since these rooms are often tucked away, they don't necessarily need to flow with the rest of the house. Earthy terracotta tones cover this room tip to tail, but with plenty of texture, it's anything but one-note. Designer Ashley Donohue mirrored the ceiling and rug using a similar shade, while a wall mural adds a moody, ethereal vibe.

Older homes can have interesting floor plans, with plenty of small nooks and cozy corners attached to main living spaces. Instead of trying to fuse those features into another room, let them become their own moment. Bookshelves, matching chairs, and a perfectly sized rug create a totally separate reading room—just far enough from the living room to feel special but close enough to be in the fray.

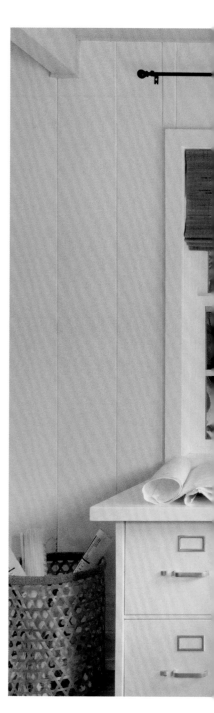

↑ A soft blue built-in is bathed in natural light, making this a great spot for a home office
   or for one of the kids to spread out some homework.

↓ Designer Jenika Kurtz turned a backyard shed into a stunning office space, complete with new windows, bright white shiplap, and plenty of storage. It required a bit of renovating but resulted in a highly functional space that was previously unusable.

↑ Hallway niches don't have to be strictly functional. In fact, if you designate a spot like this as a catchall for keys, gloves, and mail, it will be cluttered in no time. Instead, treat it like a piece of art and style it with only a few pieces you love.

← "Hallways and landing areas often can be overlooked, but they are the perfect areas to create something special," says designer Nicole Salceda of Eye for Pretty. In her San Francisco Bay Area home, she made the most of a small space she sees multiple times a day. "By adding art, a pretty vintage rug, and a weathered stool, this transition area in our home became a beautiful focal point. It makes me smile every time I walk by!"

In this nook, the coat of dark blue paint is the equivalent of a cozy blanket. A low-to-the-ground cot is the right choice for seating, giving you plenty of room between your head and the ceiling. Add loads of pillows and a spot to set your tea, and where else would you spend a snowy Sunday?

↑ Since we don't all have the luxury of an entire room that can be converted to a workspace, I'm always on the hunt for office furniture that won't look out of place. This set is located off an open concept kitchen. It blends into the wall, with some open shelving to style vases and other ceramic accessories (matching the kitchen), but closed storage hides away supplies.

← In this den, which is also used as a TV room, a freestanding desk would have taken up the entire space and eliminated the option for extra seating. Designer Amy Sklar added a custom desk into an existing bookshelf with an inlaid leather fold-down top that could be tucked away when not in use. The "photograph" is actually a Samsung Frame television that can display art when not in use.

↑ Isn't it amazing what a coat of white paint can do? This incredible home gym is above the garage. Instead of modernizing the space to match the equipment, Danny Seo styled it as he would any other room in his house. How cool is the vintage punch bowl holding the exercise ball? I love how it looks like a trophy.

↓ While the entire gym is quite impressive, my takeaway here isn't the state-of-the-art treadmill or accordion doors, but the design hack you could use in any home gym. Mirrors line the wall with a sleek ballet bar installed on top, just like at a boutique barre studio. Even if your workout space is a corner of the garage, the DIY-inclined (or a handyman) could easily install something similar. You just need a wooden dowel, wall brackets, and a specialized carbide or diamond-tipped drill bit to cut through the glass.

↑ I'll never forget the first time I toured the Novogratz's Hollywood home, a castle-style house built in 1926. This niche was discovered during demolition—it's located on a small landing in the stairwell and had been drywalled shut. They realized it would be the coolest hangout as guests made their way downstairs to the media room and transformed the "hole in the wall" into a small bar. Iconic Scalamandré wallpaper and graphic tile set the scene, with a bench to the left that's perfect for a cozy nightcap. I think it's everyone's dream to discover a hidden extra space like this in their home!

← There are a lot of scientific details that go into wine storage—temperature, humidity, light—but it can also be a striking architectural element. The velvet sofa and dark wallpaper transport me to a moody lounge in a swanky hotel lobby. For a laugh, take a closer look at the monkeys on the wallpaper. They're imbibing, too! The paper is appropriately titled Drunk Monkeys and is by Astek.

Get Organized

The most-searched topics on our website all come down to organization. Mudrooms, pantries, and laundry rooms have become some of the most satisfying rooms in the house. I think it's because they're the utilitarian spaces we find ourselves in most regularly. We spend so much time perfecting the look of our living and dining spaces, shouldn't the hardworking rooms in the house be just as lovely?

The key to designing a great laundry room is creating a space that you actually want to spend time in. If it has all the same elements as a beautiful bathroom (lovely tile, custom cabinets, sleek hardware, pretty artwork), it makes the chore feel slightly less terrible. (I said "slightly.")

If you've got room for a mudroom, take stock of the problem areas before putting together a design plan so your revamp can address a variety of needs. For instance, if everyone's bags and coats are piling up, create cubbies for each member of the family, so they know they've got a place. If you can never track down the dog's leash, have a designated hook and get in the habit of always hanging it there when you return from a walk. If there are multiple schedules to contend with on a weekly basis, a large calendar will outline who needs to be where, when.

Form can meet function in these spaces, so find ways to bring a bit of beauty to your daily routine. No guarantees you'll learn to love laundry day, but at least you can do it in a gorgeous and well-designed room.

← A long, narrow utility room feels bigger thanks to a window at the far end. A shelf with hooks can hold cleaning essentials, and a few small art pieces will give you something to look at as you fold towels for the nine hundredth time.

↑ "The homeowners wanted an oversized mudroom that was functional and organized—a single space where guests could drop their things and easily put away a pair of shoes or hang up a coat," interior designer Renee DiSanto shares. Since this house is lakeside, the use of hexagonal brick flooring means this can function as a "wet room"; kids can run in and out with wet towels, and the floor won't get too slick or messy. Cubbies were created to store towels, coolers, and gear, while a stacked washer and dryer, wash sink, and ample cabinetry add to the functionality of the space.

← When designing your dream closet, pull inspiration from your favorite department stores and boutiques. Beautiful lighting, a rug, and your favorite pieces on display will make the space feel extra special. Also, I can't say enough about matching your hangers; wood hangers are beautiful, but I'm partial to the velvet hangers you can snag at Costco. Not only are they are non-slip, but they also have a slim profile that provides more space and a uniformity that makes it easier to find your clothes.

↑ If you've got the room, I love the idea of decanting laundry detergents into glass canisters. However, it's also nice to have a few cabinets to hide away the bright packaging of stain treatment, fabric softener, and more. After all, the laundry room is a utilitarian place.

→ In this mudroom, it's all about the mirror. Though not technically a full-length mirror, it's still large enough to check your outfit on the way out the door. The mirror's large stature also makes the room feel twice as big.

→ Green mason jars house extra tealights, a few hooks grasp mugs, and vintage dishware creates an interesting color story. This space reminds me a bit of a great boutique and leads me to my number-one piece of styling advice: *How would your favorite home decor shop arrange these shelves?* In any shop, you'd find like items with like items, of course, but height, color, and texture all vary to keep your eye moving from piece to piece.

← It looks super sophisticated, but this mudroom by California designer Katie Hodges is actually a workhorse. Everything is fairly white, from the cabinetry to the overhead light: this is a clever trick to make the small room feel spacious and open. However, dark tile in a herringbone pattern expertly camouflages any dirt that's tracked in. It's the best of both worlds!

A bachelor uses this room as a bonus room. The closet to the right holds a majority of his clothes, but furniture-wise, it's just the Eames lounger. Instead of hiding his shoes away, he placed them around the perimeter of the rug alongside a few favorite art pieces. Unexpected choices like this are what I love most about being an interiors editor. At first glance, it may seem an odd choice, but it's intentional and artistic.

I've noticed that most mudrooms, like powder rooms, can be pretty bold in their design choices. But this one keeps the natural wood, both in the millwork and in the Danish-inspired bench, at the forefront. The design is entirely calm, camouflaging any potential chaos. For all you know, it could be Monica's closet (from *Friends*) behind those doors.

→ While I'd love to raid this gorgeous closet (it belongs to a successful fashion buyer), I'm looking beyond the clothes at a few smart design tricks. A valet rod can slide in and out, so you can plan outfits the night before or hang them for steaming. A slim boucle stool offers a place to sit and put on your shoes. Additional sneakers and sandals are tucked into the sliding drawers below.

↑ The details of this Vermont home acknowledge the area's long winters. With a great storage solution for cozy layers, you can quickly grab your favorite blanket on a chilly night. And when you take the time to fold them neatly, it's actually an attractive design element.

Take It Outside

Our outdoor spaces add so much value to our homes. Each is an extension of our living spaces, and this was made abundantly clear during the pandemic. As humans, we crave fresh air, a bit of vitamin D, and a change of scenery. During summer 2020, my husband and I made it our nightly routine to pour a glass of wine or iced tea and decamp to our front porch. We weren't able to hang out with our neighbors, but we could wave as they walked their dogs past. We left our phones inside, along with the endless Zooms and emails, if only for just an hour. And when we weren't catching each other up on the perils of the workday, we listened to the birds and the sounds of the children across the street splashing in their kiddie pool. By stepping outside for just a few minutes each day, we felt more connected to each other, to our community, and to the earth.

We realized the importance of this time as we searched for our first house to buy, and we slowly moved away from the dream of living right in the heart of our favorite neighborhood, around the corner from coffee shops and wine bars. Though we loved the urban environment, most houses in the area that were in our budget didn't have a proper outdoor space. We began looking for a home where we could put our feet in the grass, plant a garden, and look at the moon without one of L.A.'s famous helicopters circling overhead. Though our house-hunting journey was not for the faint of heart, we eventually found a home with a big yard, room for raised vegetable beds, and even a palm tree. A palm tree!

Whether it's a charming front porch, a spacious backyard, or a balcony off the bedroom, an outdoor space can become your own personal sanctuary. Enjoy it.

← **Who needs the pool? Two loungers and a scalloped umbrella will transport you to your favorite boutique hotel.**

Believe it or not, this isn't some bougie Palm Springs hotel; it's the backyard of a beautiful private residence. Though I love the look of tons of pillows piled on and often suggest buying pillows in varying sizes, the uniformity here creates the illusion of a custom-made cushion for the space. The fact that the pillows perfectly match the bougainvillea is just the icing on top.

With a great view, you don't need much in the way of outdoor furniture and accessories. Two comfortable chairs, a few lightweight linen blankets to wrap up in once the sun goes down, and a place to set your drink are really all you need. I grew up in Idaho, so scenes like this are all too familiar. That said, might I suggest dabbing on a little citronella or peppermint oil before heading out? It's a natural way to keep mosquitoes at bay!

One of the benefits of condo living is that it often comes with a great view. Here, opting for low-profile chairs ensures that you can appreciate the L.A. skyline while indoors—and still have a cozy seat when it's time for your sunrise coffee.

↑ The luxury of a covered patio means you can worry less about sun or water damage to your furniture. Still, the elements will find their way in. These chair cushions from Pottery Barn can be zipped off and run through the wash for easy cleanup.

The sparkling pool is the jewel of this Bay Area backyard. To match the architectural style of the house, furniture and accessories are all fairly minimal and stay within a neutral color palette.

↑ Just as you would in an open-concept home, you can create different rooms in your outdoor space using savvy furniture placement. The two butterfly chairs facing away from the dining table divide the space into two: living and dining. By having multiple areas, you will be more enticed to use the space as intended.

↑ Even in a somewhat urban setting—this backyard is located off of a kitchen in Southern California—landscaping and plants can entirely transform a space. How gorgeous are these banana leaf plants in front of the walnut slats? Without the greenery, this would just be a cement slab with some comfortable furniture. When selecting plants for your patio, I recommend taking a few pictures at different times of day so you understand the amount of natural light the space will get. Take the images when you visit your local nursery so you can get the best recommendation on what will thrive in the space. Also, pet owners, don't forget to research any plants you bring home. When ingested, many can be poisonous to cats and dogs!

← To transform your home into an indoor/outdoor oasis, floor-to-ceiling sheer window coverings will do the trick. They'll catch in the soft breeze, and suddenly the kitchen feels more like a cabana in Palm Springs. Plus, the soft light the drapes cast inside is ethereal.

↑ Designer Jenn Feldman was tasked with reimagining a unique courtyard just off a Los Angeles living room for her client, a TV writer. "She had a dream of a creative oasis where she could write, have breakfast with her kids, and enjoy wine and music at night with her husband," Feldman recalls. With the glow of a custom chandelier and the stars overhead, it's California living at its finest.

For so long, it seemed like lanterns were the only style of outdoor lighting available. Now, you can find pieces that feel less like a porch light and more like a stylish home accessory. Don't overlook this element when creating your outdoor space— there are tons of great options at all price points and styles. For something coastal, I love the pieces Regina Andrew Detroit makes, while brands like Hudson Valley Lighting have dozens of styles in everything from Modern Farmhouse to Spanish Revival. The details make the design!

← For the ultimate backyard retreat, offer a variety of seating. This space offers chairs, a loveseat, chaise lounges, and even a daybed. And for a cute styling idea, notice that the planted flowers are all clustered together to look like a big floral arrangement.

↑ A cozy cabin in the woods blends beautifully with its natural surroundings, reiterating my point of honoring your home's style and location. With its dark exterior, this is still a design-driven space, but it doesn't stand out in an obnoxious way.

→ An outdoor rug ups the cozy factor on this Manhattan Beach, California, patio—where the sea breeze can get a bit chilly. This space is great because it's right on the street, fostering a sense of community with the neighborhood. You can sit and watch the surfers stroll down to the sand.

↑ To deal with inclement weather, you need pieces that can be put away quickly. These small stools can be tucked right under the table if an unexpected rainstorm hits.

↑ The variety of pavers makes this driveway feel whimsical. Since they're confined to the center, it still looks orderly. I have to imagine it makes for a fun game of hopscotch on a hot summer's day.

↓ Even though this home is in the Georgia countryside, the boardwalk makes you feel as though you're headed to the beach. The sun-bleached wood is beautiful alongside the black exterior of the house. (And that hydrangea bush is #goals.)

↑ All that's needed to complete this scene is a pitcher of sweet tea. A swing on a covered front porch is as charming as it gets. Even though the space is protected from sun and rain, you still want to rely on outdoor fabrics for the durability of your cushions and pillows. A strong textile can protect from morning dew, pesky critters, and sticky popsicles.

↓ Ceiling fans get a bad rap, mostly because they're not quite as sexy as a well-designed light fixture. But did you know that in addition to cooling you off, fans can help deter mosquitoes and other bugs because they keep the air constantly moving? Fortunately, ceiling fans have come a long way aesthetically over the last few years. You can easily find one to match the look of your outdoor space. I suggest checking out Portland-based lighting company, Rejuvenation.

← Allow the natural landscape to help direct the set up of your outdoor space. Two palms frame this seating area beautifully.

↑ Nothing makes my heart sing more than when homes and patios are built around nature. How cute is the little palm tree cutout? If you work with a clever craftsman, you can still respect your home's natural landscaping and have your dream deck. Furniture-wise, these metal pieces can withstand the elements. Luckily, they've got a great shade cover with the trees overhead, so they shouldn't get too hot in the summer.

↑ If you've got a view of your outdoor furniture from the interior, be mindful to choose pieces that complement the style inside—it's an extension of your living space and should flow as such.

← Don't feel limited by one statement piece or wreath. Instead you can think outside of the box when it comes to front porch decor. If it's a covered space, try your hand at curating a little gallery wall, add a shelf for trinkets, or display small sculptures. Let your personality shine!

↑ Here's just a small patio off the primary bedroom. By adding an outdoor soaker tub and a shower, you're transported to the spa. The fence is extended a few feet vertically for privacy.

→ Adirondacks are a classic, all-American chair—originally designed by Thomas Lee in 1903 in Westport, New York. Today, they are made in a variety of hardy materials, the most durable being a high-density polyethylene, which is made to withstand the elements. This material tends to be more costly, but the chairs will stand the test of time year after year.

Acknowledgments

When I received the call that I'd be writing this book, I burst into tears and then laughter and then more tears. Writing a book is a lifelong dream realized, but I'm keenly aware that I wouldn't have this opportunity without the support of both my professional and personal communities. I have so many people to thank.

My husband, Tim, has supported me in every sense of the word over the last decade, from encouraging me to pursue my dreams to supporting me financially when those dreams were less than lucrative. He has manned the espresso machine each morning and quietly put dinner on my desk on the days I worked late into the night. Most of all, he has made me laugh every single day.

My dad, John Ryder, drove me to every writing camp in the Treasure Valley and has provided unwavering support in every venture, from the time I wanted to be a drummer in a punk rock band to my questionable soccer skills. I can't wait for you to hold this book! My mom, Sue, carefully edited every school paper and showed me by example that nothing should stand in the way of my goals. My stepmom, Debi, has been the constant sunshine in our lives. My brother, Jake, is way smarter and funnier than I am and has always watched over me, both protecting me in a way only big brothers can and encouraging me to push the creative boundaries. And Aunt Karen and Aunt Donna have influenced and guided me more than they know.

Crystal Palecek, the visionary who started Rue more than ten years ago, and the entire founding team, built an incredible foundation, and I am so grateful to carry the torch into the new chapter. Mandy Mortimer has been my right-hand gal for so many years and my biggest cheerleader as one chapter ended and a new one began. Victoria de la Camara, Kat McEachern, Julie Edwards, Maia McDonald Smith, and everyone who was involved in those early years of Rue, I am so grateful to have worked alongside you, especially on those late nights in Oakland as we readied another issue.

Danny Seo saw my potential and gave me the opportunity of a lifetime. Thank you for bringing Rue to print and helping to shepherd the brand into a new era. Most of all, though, thank you for being a fantastic friend, business partner, and mentor. I am so grateful to learn from you each day. None of this would be possible without you and your vision.

For this new chapter: Barry Rosenbloom trusted our vision and gave us free reign to create something new, and the entire team at RFP Corporation keeps the wheels turning. Michael Wilson and Alexis Cook at Made Visible Studio and Sandra S. Soria lent their vision and patience as we launched our first print issue, which put new meaning to the phrase "my first rodeo." My friend and publicist pro, Noelle Smith Primavera, you're such a bright light in each day! Rich Pedine was the ultimate problem solver and brings laughter to every Friday. And my dear friend Amy Bartlam helped me bring this book from the base of the mountain right to the top.

My book agent Joy Tutela at David Black Agency helped bring this book to the right team at Ten Speed Press. Without your expertise and encouragement, I would likely still be plugging away at the proposal. My editor Dervla Kelly—I am so grateful to you for seeing the potential in our concept (and me!) and fine-tuning all of my ideas. I am so thankful to have you in my corner. My designer Betsy Stromberg—this book would be nothing without your creative vision. My production editor, Kim Keller; production manager, Jane Chinn; marketer, Andrea Portanova; and publicist, Lauren Kretzschmar—it is a thrill to work with such a talented team and a lifelong dream to partner with such a prestigious publisher.

To the many designers, photographers, and publicists who make my job easy. Thank you for lending your expertise and talent to Rue over the years and, most of all, to this book. I am so proud of the community we've created. And a very special thank you to designer Kristen Peña and photographer R. Brad Knipstein for sharing your exquisite work on our cover.

Finally, I'd be remiss to leave out Mike Spaulding, a job recruiter turned lifelong friend. While reviewing my résumé over beers on a sunny afternoon in Boise, Idaho, he planted the seed that I could leave my unfulfilling corporate career behind and make a living out of my passion for writing and beautiful design. Without his suggestion, I never would have found my way to Rue.

Resources

Bedding and Bath

Bolé Road
www.boleroadtextiles.com

Coyuchi
www.coyuchi.com

Cultiver
www.cultiver.com

Matteo
www.matteola.com

Morrow Soft Goods
www.morrowsoftgoods.com

Linoto
www.linoto.com

Parachute
www.parachutehome.com

Pom Pom at Home
www.pompomathome.com

Weezie Towels
www.weezietowels.com

Decor and Accessories

54 Kibo
www.54kibo.com

Anastasio Home
www.anastasiohome.com

Anyon Atelier
www.anyondesign.com

Bloomist
www.bloomist.com

FAVOR
www.infavorof.com

GARDE
www.gardeshop.com

Goodee
www.goodeeworld.com

Jungalow by Justina Blakeney
www.jungalow.com

Nickey Kehoe
www.nickeykehoe.com

OKA
www.oka.com

St. Frank
www.stfrank.com

Fabrics and Textiles

ALT for Living
www.altforliving.com

Bassett McNab
www.bassettmcnab.com

Caroline Cecil Textiles
www.carolinececiltextiles.com

Cloth & Company
www.clothandcompany.com

Crypton
www.crypton.com

Hollywood at Home
www.hollywoodathome.com

Susan Connor New York
www.susanconnorny.com

Furniture

Arhaus
www.arhaus.com

Cisco Home
www.ciscohome.net

Croft House
www.crofthouse.com

Industry West
www.industrywest.com

Lawson-Fenning
www.lawsonfenning.com

Living Spaces
www.livingspaces.com

Jayson Home
www.jaysonhome.com

Maker&Son
www.makerandson.us

Noir
www.noirfurniturela.com

Palecek
www.palecek.com

Sawkille Co.
www.sawkille.com

Universal
www.universalfurniture.com

Kitchen and Tabletop

Cocktail Kingdom
www.cocktailkingdom.com

Estelle Colored Glass
www.estellecoloredglass.com

etúHome
www.etuhome.com

Fable
www.fablehome.co

Hudson Grace
www.hudsongracesf.com

Leeway Home
www.leewayhome.co

Mud Australia
www.mudaustralia.com

Jono Pandolfi
www.jonopandolfi.com

MARCH
www.marchsf.com

Soho Home
www.sohohome.com

Lighting

Apparatus Studio
www.apparatusstudio.com

Articolo
www.articololighting.com

Cedar & Moss
www.cedarandmoss.com

Currey & Company
www.curreyandcompany.com

Hinkley
www.hinkley.com

Original BTC
www.us.originalbtc.com

Regina Andrew Detroit
www.reginaandrew.com

Schoolhouse
www.schoolhouse.com

Urban Electric
www.urbanelectric.com

workstead
www.workstead.com

Rugs

Aelfie
www.aelfie.com

Armadillo
www.usa.armadillo-co.com

Beni Rugs
www.benirugs.com

Jaipur
www.jaipurliving.com

Lulu & Georgia
www.luluandgeorgia.com

Loloi
www.loloirugs.com

Merida
www.meridastudio.com

Nordic Knots
www.nordicknots.com

The Rug Company
www.therugcompany.com

Tile and Stone

Ann Sacks
www.annsacks.com

Artistic Tile
www.artistictile.com

Cambria
www.cambriausa.com

clé tile
www.cletile.com

Country Floors
www.countryfloors.com

Granada Tile
www.granadatile.com

Heath Ceramics
www.heathceramics.com

Wall Coverings

A Street Prints
www.astreetprints.com

Chasing Paper
www.chasingpaper.com

l'aviva home
www.lavivahome.com

Manuka Textiles
www.manukatextiles.com

Mitchell Black
www.mitchellblack.com

Rebecca Atwood
www.rebeccaatwood.com

Sheila Bridges
www.sheilabridges.com

Window Treatments

Everhem
www.everhem.com

Hartmann&Forbes
www.hartmannforbes.com

Hunter Douglas
www.hunterdouglas.com

The Shade Store
www.theshadestore.com

Credits

Interior Design Credits

Gabrielle Aker, Aker Interiors: Foreword, 46, 108, 132, 146, 147, 148, 238, 256

Sarah Birnie, Sarah Birnie Interiors: 42, 43, 80, 134

Rebecca Cartwright: 31, 78, 136, 229

Rita Chan, Rita Chan Interiors: 29, 63, 96, 154, 180

Erin Chelius, Chelius House of Design: 144

Megan D'Amour and Sabrina Speer, D2 Interiors: 90, 91, 226

Heath Daughtry and Sunny Whang Daughtry: 112, 162, 244, 245, 247

Jesse DeSanti, Jette Creative: Title Page, Introduction, 20, 33, 34, 68, 95, 140, 205, 234

Renee DiSanto and Christina Samatas, Park & Oak Interior Design: 13, 194, 217

Ashley Donohue, Ashley Donohue Design: 152, 155, 198

Donna DuFresne, Donna DuFresne Interior Design: 18

Jenn Feldman, Jenn Feldman Designs: 172, 237

Jessica Fleming and Devon McKeon, Hive LA Home: Dedication Page, 60, 62, 73, 92, 93, 153, 200, 230

Sandra Fox, Sandra Fox Interiors: 173, 176, 232

Casey Gerber and Tarryn Meghan, Two/Tone Interiors: 79, 160

Linda Hayslett, L.H. Designs: 190

India Hicks: 15, 77, 81, 135

Katie Hodges, Katie Hodges Design: 56, 102, 103, 142, 170, 178, 220

Stewart Horner, Penny Black Interiors: 16

Max Humphrey: 26, 122, 166

Clara Jung, Banner Day Interiors: 117, 169, 182

Maayan Kessler, Maayan Kessler Design: 24, 104, 158, 189, 225

Jenika Kurtz, J. Kurtz Design: 203

Montana Labelle, Montana Labelle Design: 28, 38, 64, 113, 124, 126, 157

Tiffany Leigh, Tiffany Leigh Design: 25, 59, 67, 128, 219

Kate Lester, Kate Lester Interiors: 11, 61, 71, 119, 149, 159, 202, 243

Jodi Levine: 88

Alessia Zanchi Loffredo and Sarah Coscarelli, reDesign Home: 44, 45, 100, 101, 106, 107, 199

Johanna Lowe: 139

Genna Margolis, SHAPESIDE: 109, 163, 188, 209, 251

Veronica Martin and Carrie Stinson, Two Fold Interiors: 8, 9, 22, 48, 75, 86, 87, 127, 133, 223

Ashley Montgomery, Ashley Montgomery Design: 89, 150, 151, 181

Jules Moore: 30, 74, 137, 228, 248

Laura Muller, Four Point Design Build: 32

Emilie Munroe, Studio Munroe: 19, 40, 70, 118, 130, 131, 168, 193

Bob and Cortney Novogratz, The Novogratz: 41, 83, 110, 177, 185, 186, 192, 213, 253

Patrick Pastella: 14, 49, 51, 111, 224

Kristen Peña, K Interiors: 4, 7, 54, 55, 94, 120, 129, 141, 143, 211, 212, 252

Joyce Downing Pickens, JDP Interiors: 156

Cisco Pinedo: 53, 242, 249

Tricia Rose: 114

Nicole Salceda, Eye for Pretty: 204, 214, 216, 218, 233

Amanda Schuon: 10, 27, 183

Danny Seo: 17, 138, 195, 206, 210, 221, 241, 250

Patrick and Megan Sharp, Mister + Mrs Sharp: 36, 47, 58, 240

Amy Sklar, Amy Sklar Design: 116, 164, 167, 208

Stacie Stukin: 66, 161

Lauren Svenstrup, Studio Sven: 12, 72, 76, 84

Laura Umansky, Laura U Design Collective: 37, 174, 179

Jennifer Vaquero, September Workshop: 165, 196

Brooke Wagner, Brooke Wagner Design: 50, 99, 184, 197

Lada Webster, squarefoot interior design: 6, 39, 98, 222, 235, 236

Holly Williams: 246

Photography Credits

Amy Bartlam: Title Page, Dedication Page, Foreword, Introduction, 6, 11, 20, 29, 32, 33, 34, 37, 39, 46, 56, 60, 61, 62, 63, 68, 71, 73, 79, 90, 91, 92, 93, 95, 96, 98, 102, 103, 108, 109, 116, 119, 132, 140, 142, 144, 146, 147, 148, 149, 152, 153, 154, 155, 156, 159, 160, 163, 164, 165, 167, 170, 172, 173, 174, 176, 178, 179, 180, 188, 196, 198, 200, 202, 203, 204, 205, 208, 209, 214, 216, 218, 220, 222, 226, 230, 232, 233, 234, 235, 236, 237, 238, 243, 251, 254

Christopher Dibble: 16, 18, 26, 122, 166

Renee DiSanto: 13, 194, 217

David Engelhardt: 14, 15, 31, 36, 47, 49, 51, 58, 77, 78, 81, 88, 111, 135, 136, 195, 210, 224, 229, 240

Alexandra Grablewski: 114

Jonas Jungblut: 10, 21, 27, 30, 50, 52, 53, 66, 74, 82, 99, 112, 115, 137, 139, 161, 162, 183, 184, 197, 228, 242, 244, 245, 247, 248, 249

R. Brad Knipstein: Cover, 4, 7, 54, 55, 94, 120, 129, 141, 143, 211, 212, 252

Thomas Kuoh: 19, 40, 70, 118, 130, 131, 168, 193

Staci Marengo: 41, 192, 213

Ryan McDonald: 12, 44, 45, 72, 76, 84, 100, 101, 106, 107, 199

Lauren Miller: 8, 9, 22, 24, 25, 28, 38, 42, 43, 48, 59, 64, 67, 75, 80, 86, 87, 89, 104, 113, 124, 126, 127, 128, 133, 134, 150, 151, 157, 158, 181, 189, 219, 223, 225

The Novogratz: 185

Lauren Pressey: 190

Colin Price: 117, 169, 182

Armando Rafael: 17, 138, 206, 221, 241, 250

Matt Wier: 246

Matthew Williams: 83, 110, 177, 186, 253

Library of Congress Cataloging-in-Publication Data
  Names: Lamb, Kelli, author. | Berkus, Nate, writer of foreword.
  Title: Home with Rue : style for everyone / by Kelli Lamb;
    foreword by Nate Berkus.
  Other titles: Rue.
  Description: First edition. | California : Ten Speed Press, [2022] | Includes index.
  Identifiers: LCCN 2021039909 (print) | LCCN 2021039910 (ebook) | ISBN 9781984860682
    (hardcover) | ISBN 9781984860699 (ebook)
  Subjects: LCSH: Interior decoration—Themes, motives.
  Classification: LCC NK2110 .L34 2022 (print) | LCC NK2110 (ebook) | DDC 747—dc23
  LC record available at https://lccn.loc.gov/2021039909
  LC ebook record available at https://lccn.loc.gov/2021039910

Hardcover ISBN: 978-1-9848-6068-2
eBook ISBN: 978-1-9848-6069-9

Printed in China

Editor: Dervla Kelly | Production editor: Kim Keller | Editorial assistant: Zoey Brandt
Art director and designer: Betsy Stromberg | Production designer: Mari Gill
Typefaces: DSType's Acta, Zetafonts's Blacker Sans Pro
Production manager: Jane Chinn
Prepress color manager: Nicholas Patton
Copyeditor: Amy Bauman | Proofreader: Lisa Brousseau
Publicist: Lauren Kretzschmar | Marketer: Andrea Portanova

10 9 8 7 6 5 4 3 2 1

First Edition